Charles Bullock

Bible Inspiration

What is, and what is not

Charles Bullock

Bible Inspiration
What is, and what is not

ISBN/EAN: 9783337114114

Printed in Europe, USA, Canada, Australia, Japan

Cover: Foto ©Lupo / pixelio.de

More available books at **www.hansebooks.com**

"THE PENTATEUCH AND BISHOP COLENSO."

BIBLE INSPIRATION;

WHAT IT IS, AND WHAT IT IS NOT:

DR. COLENSO'S DIFFICULTIES CONSIDERED:

AND

OUR LORD'S TESTIMONY ENFORCED.

BY THE
REV. CHARLES BULLOCK,

Rector of Saint Nicholas, Worcester; Author of "The Way Home,"
"The Syrian Leper," etc.

"It is the Bible or it is no Bible."
DR. CHALMERS.

From contempt of Thy Word and Commandment,
Good Lord deliver us.
LITANY.

THIRD EDITION.

LONDON:
WERTHEIM, MACINTOSH, AND HUNT;
AND
STRAHAN AND CO.
WORCESTER:
EATON AND SON, AND ALL BOOKSELLERS.

1863.

CONTENTS.

—

PRAYER.

"Blessed Lord, who hast caused ALL Holy Sriptures to be written for our learning; Grant that we may in such wise hear them, read, mark, learn, and inwardly digest them, that by patience, and comfort of THY HOLY WORD, we may embrace and ever hold fast the blessed hope of everlasting life, which Thou hast given us in our Saviour Jesus Christ. Amen."

"That it may please Thee to illuminate all Bishops, Priests, and Deacons, with true knowledge and understanding of THY WORD, and that both by their preaching and living they may set it forth, and show it accordingly :

"We beseech Thee to hear us, good Lord.

"That it may please Thee to give to all Thy people increase of grace to hear meekly THY WORD, and to receive it with pure affection, and to bring forth the fruits of the Spirit :

"We beseech Thee to hear us, good Lord."

Litany.

BIBLE INSPIRATION;

WHAT IT IS, AND WHAT IT IS NOT:

DR. COLENSO'S DIFFICULTIES CONSIDERED:

AND

OUR LORD'S TESTIMONY ENFORCED.

INTRODUCTION.

The occasion which has led to the publication of the following pages is one of sad and painful interest. A Bishop of our Church has publicly avowed himself a champion of scepticism. Dr. Colenso, Bishop of Natal, has published a book on the Pentateuch* which, if its conclusions were admitted, however the writer may at present endeavour to qualify them, would effectually rob us of our faith in the Bible as God's Revelation to man.

When we bear in mind the position held—still held by Dr. Colenso, Bishop in a Church whose office it is to be "a witness and a keeper of Holy Writ," † we may well be startled and amazed. Our surprise at his avowal of unbelief in the infallible authority of the Bible, is only equalled by our surprise at the moral obliquity of judgment which can allow him to continue to hold his post of dignity and receive its emoluments. Carefully does it become us, writing on topics which stir the heart to its depths, to guard against remarks which might seem uncharitable towards an individual. But Dr. Colenso's *official* responsibility demands an emphatic protest from every true Churchman. And without contemplating any steps that may be taken by those in

---

* The Pentateuch and Book of Joshua, critically examined. Longman and Co., 1862.

† Article xx.

authority to vindicate, in the name of the Church, the violation of his Ordination compact, we may safely say, that his *incredulity* in rejecting the historical veracity of the Pentateuch on the grounds advanced in the volume he has written, irrespective of—nay, ignoring altogether the positive Christian evidences external and internal,—is on a par with his *credulity*, if he really believes that it is possible for him, after the avowal of his scepticism, to retain with a quiet conscience, both his office, and his moral consistency in the judgment of the community at large.*

But apart from personal and ecclesiastical considerations, the publication of Dr. Colenso's book has aroused a spirit of anxious and earnest enquiry in the minds of many who have hitherto, as believers in the Divine Inspiration and Authority of the Bible, reposed in confidence on the judgment of the universal Church represented by men eminent alike for scholarship and piety. Our people are turning to their ministers,—justly turning to them, as men pledged by the most solemn vow to use " all faithful diligence to banish and drive away all erroneous and strange doctrines contrary to God's Word," †—and they ask us for information which may serve them as armour of defence against the assaults of scepticism and unbelief,—information which may enable them, with the assurance of enlightened conviction, to "give an answer to every man that asketh them a reason for the hope that is in them." (1 Peter iii., 15.) ‡

---

* The writer may refer the reader to a Lecture given in Worcester, on the publication of the "Essays and Reviews," in which this question of moral consistency is fully discussed. "Essays and Reviews: The False Position of the Authors: An Appeal to the Bible and Prayer Book." Wertheim and Co.

† Service for the Ordination of Presbyters or Priests.

‡ "To respond to this call is clearly a solemn ministerial duty. No doubt, as a general rule, it is best to let poisonous literature alone. It is best to set truth before us, and act out the truth we know: and in every such case we shall find our love of truth a sure preservative against the subtle influences of error. The royal law of God's kingdom of truth, will vindicate itself in our happy experience,—'If any man will do the will of God, he shall know of the doctrine whether it be of God.' (St. John vii., 17.) But we must not *always* let error alone. We may *prefer* to do so, but it would-be the indulgence of a dangerous preference, if the result should be an impression on the minds of the undecided, that we are silent because we have nothing to say, or because we fear the discussion might have an unfavourable issue. Silence now, I am convinced, might lead to such an impression. I have cause to know that it *has* done so in

Of course, a pamphlet cannot embrace and answer the allegations of a volume, and the thought may occur to some, as it occurred to me, would it not be better to wait for the issue of the works now in preparation, which will contain full and satisfactory refutations of Dr. Colenso's book. I weighed this consideration, and certainly if I had reason to hope that the circulation of these *complete* answers would be co-extensive with the circulation of the poisonous errors promulgated in Dr. Colenso's volume, I should have deemed a pamphlet out of place. But I am well-persuaded that the circulation of *books* in answer to Dr. Colenso, will not meet the *present* and *pressing* necessities of the case. The circulation of the books, about to be published, will be limited : the circulation of Dr. Colenso's errors is already world-wide. His book, indeed, has, at present, fallen into comparatively few hands,—although we hear of ten thousand copies being disposed of in five days,—but we all know that, through the medium of the press, the entire reading population has been put in possession of *extracts*, conveying the pith and marrow of the volume. I cannot but feel that the circulation of these *extracts*, unaccompanied with any refutation, and in some instances followed by expressions of sympathy and approval,* is likely to produce far more injurious and pernicious results than the circulation of Dr. Colenso's book itself. Those who read the book, will most probably read the volumes written in answer to it; but the large majority of those who read the *extracts*, will neither read the book nor its replies.

Acting upon these convictions, I have thought that a pamphlet, aiming to supply in a plain and popular form, an antidote to the

some instances. I conclude, therefore, that the obligations of ministerial duty imperatively require us, in these days, to 'contend,' and contend 'earnestly ' too, ' for the faith once delivered to the saints.' We must do what we can to counteract the undermining process which is being carried on by (so-called) Rationalistic teachers. We must aim to 'stablish, strengthen, settle' our people, 'building them up upon the foundation of the apostles and prophets, Jesus Christ Himself being the chief corner stone.' (Jude, 3, 1 Pet. **v.**, 10, Eph. ii., 20.)"—"Essays and Reviews : The False Position, &c." P. 4.

* The *Daily Telegraph*, boasting of a circulation exceeding that of the *Times* and all the other London daily papers put together, has thus employed its responsible influence. Let heads of households look to the papers they place in the hands of the young. Poison is easily imbibed.

poison of scepticism, *as it is administered in these* EXTRACTS, might be of service, although I could not address myself to the *detailed* consideration of Dr. Colenso's book as a whole.

The object I have in view, thus defined, I propose, in my endeavour to obtain that object :—

I.—To offer a few general remarks on the question of BIBLE INSPIRATION—WHAT IT IS, AND WHAT IT IS NOT :—

II.—To point out THE FALLACY OF SOME OF THE PRINCIPAL DIFFICULTIES AND OBJECTIONS ADVANCED BY DR. COLENSO.

III.—To commend as the very pivot of the whole controversy OUR LORD'S CONCLUSIVE TESTIMONY TO THE INSPIRATION OF THE PENTATEUCH; and in conclusion :—

IV.—To press upon my readers THE MOMENTOUS PRACTICAL BEARINGS OF THE SUBJECT.

I.

BIBLE INSPIRATION—WHAT IT IS, AND WHAT IT IS NOT.

Accurate ideas of the nature and boundaries of BIBLE INSPIRATION, will materially assist us in estimating Dr. Colenso's work.

I would request attention to three leading observations, which I think will embrace, if they they do not exactly express, the orthodox view of Bible Inspiration—what it is, and what it is not.

1. *Bible Inspiration* IS A FACT—*independently of the various theories by which the attempt has been made to define it.* Whether the Inspiration be Plenary or Verbal, Dynamical or Mechanical, THE BIBLE IS INSPIRED. It is of Divine Origin and Authority. The Canonical Scriptures, as they proceeded at first from the inspired penmen, were written by men whose minds were, at the time, under the immediate control of the Holy Spirit: so that, whilst they expressed themselves in the words and idioms which as individuals they ordinarily used, they nevertheless expressed only, neither more nor less, what God would have them express.

2. *Bible Inspiration does not exclude what has been fitly termed
" The Human Element in Scripture."* As a *written* Revelation
this element could not be excluded. Hence, on examining the
Bible, we find that the gift of Inspiration admitted in the sacred
writers of diligent and faithful research (Luke i., 1-4), of the
expression of the same thought in different words, (Compare Matt.
xxvi., 26, 27 : Luke xxii., 19, 20, and I Cor. xi., 24, 25,
and Matt. iii., 17 ; Mark i., 11, and Luke iii., 22,) of such
differences (not discrepancies) between the accounts of inspired
men as would be likely to arise from the different stand-points of
each, (many instances occur in the Gospel,) of quotations from
other inspired authorities, (Psa. cviii. and Psa. lvii., 7-11,
lx., 5-12 : Gen. x. xi., and 1 Chron. i., 17, etc : 2 Kings
xviii., 13-37, and Isa. xxxvi., 1-22,) of the employment of
uninspired documents, (Josh. x., 13, Numb. xxi., 14 : Jude.
ix., 14, 15,) and of peculiarities of style and manner arising from
diversities of intellectual structure, and from educational or other
influences, such as may be observed on a comparison of Ezekiel
and Isaiah, of John and Paul. This human element may also
be recognised in the *transmission* of the Bible. Hence :—*

3. *The Inspiration of the Bible is not synonymous with entire
freedom from the intrusion of the slightest error in the translations
and versions which we possess, made from copies of the first original
autographs.* Translations, however trustworthy, are not completely
perfect. In so large a work, *numbers* and *names in the genealogies,*
are peculiarly liable to suffer from successive transcriptions.
" Every biblical scholar will readily admit, that the Inspiration of
the Bible does not secure, as it does not require, theoretic and
mathematical freedom from error, when it reaches the great bulk of
its readers and fulfils its great practical object as a Revelation to
mankind."†

Now, it will be evident to every reader of Dr. Colenso's work,
that he has been unable to grasp the subject of Bible Inspiration

---

* See Note. p. 51.
† " The Bible and Modern Thought." By the Rev. T. R. Birks, M.A.
Religious Tract Society. A volume of *inestimable* value. The writer cannot too
strongly urge every reader to obtain it. It is published in a cheap form,

in these, its primary aspects. He tells us that " the creed of the school in which he was educated," required him to " reverence every word—every *letter* of the Bible " (the Bible *in our translation*) " as the Word of God, the direct utterance of the Most High." " In those days," he continues, " I was taught that it was my duty to fling the suggestion"—that there might be minor errors or mis-statements *in our translation*, without in the least detracting from the real value of the book—" I was taught to fling this " suggestion from me at once, ' as if it were a loaded shell, shot " into the fortress of my soul.' " It would have been well for Dr. Colenso, if he had rejected the teaching of this school, of which there are surely few disciples, and sought counsel in the standard works of the Christian Church. But he has rushed from one extreme to the other. Failing to recognise THE HUMAN ELEMENT influencing the *transmission* of Scripture, he has allowed his mind to dwell—morbidly to dwell—upon the minor difficulties inseparable from that human element, till the pressure of these difficulties— *magnified and re-magnified to his absorbed gaze*—has led him to take the fatal step of rejecting the essentially DIVINE ELEMENT.

" God is my witness !" he exclaims, " what hours of wretched- " ness have I spent at times, while reading the Bible, and " reverencing every word of it as the Word of God, when petty " contradictions met me which seemed to my reason to conflict " with the notion of the absolute historical veracity of every part " of Scripture."

A Reviewer, quoting this painful passage, aptly puts the question, " Where was the occasion for all this wretchedness ?" Where indeed ! Every real difficulty would have quickly dis-appeared had he borne in mind the human as well as the Divine Element in Revelation.

The Reviewer continues :—" The sacred writers are, to use " Archbishop Ussher's illustration, ' God's Secretaries.' He leaves " them real men, capable of giving honest and reliable testimony, " like any other men, but He carefully watches over them so that " not one untrue or improper word shall be given forth in His " name. When an earthly sovereign desires his secretary to write " a letter in his name, he will take care that the letter, when

" written, shall faithfully express his meaning :—yet there may bo
" one or two immaterial imperfections in the document of which he
" does not care to take notice."*

These are forcible and weighty words. The analogy is exactly
to the point. The relative position of the Divine and human
elements in Scripture, is at once seen. Throughout the sacred
volume GoD speaks to us, and this fact assures us that the Bible
is ALL TRUE. But it is equally a fact that, throughout the Bible
men like ourselves speak to us, and we receive the Bible in a
translated form. We therefore expect to find, mingled with its
Divine element, and in a measure affecting its transmission from
age to age, the presence of the human element. All that we are
careful to assert is, that this human element does not, IN THE
. LEAST, interfere with the Inspiration—the Divine Origin and
Authority—of the Bible. We do not say the sacred text has
been miraculously preserved from the trifling mistakes of successive
copyists or transcribers : but it is not the less GOD's BOOK : and
in His good Providence, employing the instrumentality of human
care and watchfulness, we believe it has been secured from any
errors or interpolations of importance. The result of the
unwearied toil of critics and philologists, examining and comparing all existing versions, is a triumphant testimony to *the
almost perfect integrity of the text as we have it.* Jew and Christian,
Romanist and Protestant, have been mutual checks : and their
agreement as to the letter of the Bible is an evident token of its
purity. Dr. Moses Stuart, referring to the various " readings "
of which learned men often speak, remarks, —" All these taken
" together do not change or materially affect any important point
" of doctrine, precept, or even history."†

* *Christian Observer* for December. Pp. 922-3. The writer wishes to
acknowledge his obligations to this masterly Review of Dr. Colenso's work. He
would also recommend the reader to obtain the Reprint of the *Record* Reviews.
A more *thorough* refutation could not be desired. The writer has been indebted
to it in several instances.

† " The mistake of a letter or word by a copyist, or the change of meaning
" attached to some word, will frequently remove a difficulty or apparent discrepancy
" in Scripture. For instance, Paine asks scoffingly, whether the spoiling of the
" Egyptians by the Israelites was not an immoral transaction, and whether the
" statement that the 'borrowing' on the part of the Israelites was by the Divine

12

Such, then, are our ideas of the nature and the boundaries of
BIBLE INSPIRATION. We say the Bible is GOD'S BOOK—God's
Word—a Revelation of His mind and will, conveyed to us in the
form He in His wisdom saw fit to adopt—and certainly that form
is A TRUTHFUL FORM.

And here we are at direct variance with Dr. Colenso. He tells
us, indeed,—and we are ready to exclaim " the voice is the voice
of Jacob,"—that he " believes unfeignedly in the Divine authority
of the Scriptures,"—that he " believes the Inspiration of the
Holy One breathes throughout its pages,"—that he " relies on
the records as an efficient instrument of communication from God
to man in all that is necessary to salvation,"—that he is anxious
to " give due honour to the book as containing a message from
God to our souls," as, in fact, " the very Book of Truth :"*—but
then, however unaccountable it may seem to plain readers, he
professes with the same breath, to have discovered in this " very
Book of Truth," " a series of manifest, absolute, palpable, self-
contradictions and inconsistencies,"—the narrative of the Exodus
being " full of contradictions, and plain impossibilities, affecting
the entire substance of the story."†

The disproof of these assertions we shall give presently: but
we say, at once, we reject as MOST IMPIOUS the conclusion, to
which Dr. Colenso is inevitably committed,—namely—that God's
Revelation of Himself and of His Will is conveyed to us in a
Book abounding in historical falsehoods. *What should we think*

" command, does not implicate the Divine Being in an act of dishonesty? A
" reference to any good Commentary would have shown him that the word used
" by Moses presents no difficulty whatever. The Egyptians were urgent to get
" rid of the people, and eagerly, at their request, *gave* of their property. The
" word rendered ' borrowed,' in the original is simply ' asked.' Thus Hannah
" is said to have ' asked ' for Samuel, and to have ' lent,' *i.e., given* ' him to the
" ' Lord.' The trifling variations in the Gospels are capable of similar explana-
" tion. In point of fact, this *circumstantial variety* is a proof of *substantial*
" *truth*. A close and minute agreement of professed independent witnesses
" induces the suspicion of confederacy and fraud,—whereas apparent, though
" trifling discrepancies, are real and conclusive proof of independent testimony.
" Thus, as Pascal observes, ' Even the apparently *weak* points in the chain of
" ' evidence have their *peculiar force* to a well-constituted mind.' " Essays and
Reviews. The False Position of the Authors: an Appeal to the Bible and the
Prayer Book. Pp. 34, 35.

* Pp. 150, 151, 152. Pref., xxxiii. † Pp. 10, 11, 17, 141.

*of a man who told us lies that he might mix up truth—a measure
of truth with the lies?* Awful as the blasphemy must appear to
the reverential mind, this is the position of those who talk, as
Dr. Colenso talks, of receiving the *teaching* of the Bible, whilst
rejecting the *truth of the narratives* contained in the Bible. Both
stand or fall together.

Even Dr. Colenso cannot altogether blind himself to the fact,
that this must be the final result. He seems almost to anticipate
and prepare for it, since he tells us, that—" Our belief in the
Living God would remain as sure as ever though not the
Pentateuch only, but the *whole Bible*, were removed :" and that
" It is, perhaps, God's will that we shall be taught in this our
day, among other precious lessons, not to build our faith upon a
Book, though it be the Bible itself, but to realise more truly the
blessedness of knowing that He Himself is nearer and dearer to
us than any book can be,—that His Voice within the heart may
be heard continually by the obedient child that listens for it, and
that shall be our Teacher and Guide, in the path of duty, which
is the path of life, when all other helpers—even the words of the
best of Books—may fail us."*

It might have occurred to Dr. Colenso to ask himself what
this " hearing of God's Voice within the heart " has done for the
heathen world, bereft of any written Revelation of God's Will ?
St. Paul has given an answer, which the modern experience of
missionaries too sadly confirms. (Rom. I.) We cannot but
reflect, that, but for the privilege of a Scriptural education, Dr.
Colenso, in spite of this " Voice of God within the heart," might
at this moment, as a poor idolater, have needed one to teach him
the elementary Bible truth—There *is* a God !

But keeping to the point before us, these quotations from Dr.
Colenso's work make it very clear, that whatever words he may
employ, " in *some* sense,"† to express his " unfeigned faith in
the Divine Authority of the Scriptures," his present hold upon the

---

teaching of the Bible is not likely to be a tenacious or a lasting hold.

For ourselves, adopting the orthodox view of Bible Inspiration, we simply urge, that it is *impossible* to separate the historical narratives of the Bible from its teaching. These narratives are of such a matter of fact character, and moreover so plainly assert miraculous agency in connection with the teaching of the Book, that if we reject the facts consistency demands the rejection of the teaching also. The truth of the teaching depends on the truth of the narrative. We are pledged to the truthfulness of the narrative, if we acknowledge the authority of the teaching. To profess to revere the one, whilst we falsify the other, is to take hold of the Bible with the hand of pretended friendship the more effectually to stab it to the heart. A God of Truth could only reveal Himself to us by means of a truthful Book. If the Bible be a Divinely Inspired Revelation it must be TRUTHFUL.

II.

SCEPTICAL DIFFICULTIES ADVANCED BY DR. COLENSO.

This is our second topic. Dr. Colenso professes to have found, in the Pentateuch, " a series of manifest, absolute, palpable self-contradictions, inconsistencies, and impossibilities." The preceding pages will enable my readers to judge of the extraordinary inconsistency, of which he convicts himself, when, after thus charging falsehood upon the Bible—falsehood upon narratives which claim to be literal and historical, and have always been so received by the universal Church,—he tells us that "he is not conscious of having said anything which contravenes the solemn profession of his Ordination vow—' I do unfeignedly believe in all the Canonical Scriptures.' "*

But leaving Dr. Colenso to account to the Church, and to his own conscience, for his inconsistency, the question with which we are concerned is this,—has he, really, found in the Pentateuch, " a series of manifest, absolute, palpable self-contradictions,

* Preface. P. xxxiii.

inconsistencies, and impossibilities ?" Without a moment's hesitation, the believer in the Inspiration of the Bible may reply —he has not. If, indeed, Dr. Colenso could bind us down to a theory of Inspiration entirely precluding the "human element" —of which we have spoken—(precluding in truth *written* Revelation altogether)—then, no doubt, in the translated Bible which we possess, an erroneous figure here, and a mistaken name there, might be said to be irreconcilable with *that* theory. But the Bible Inspiration for which we contend *allows* the existence of this "human element,"—accounting for divergencies in the composition, and trivial errors in the transmission, of the Bible,— and we are prepared to maintain that Dr. Colenso has utterly failed to allege any difficulties which ought to shake our belief in the five books of Moses, as a Divine record of events which actually occurred as they are narrated on the sacred page. He has, in fact, said very little that is new, beyond his arithmetical calculations. We have his own confession—" I am well aware that most of the points here considered have been already brought forward by various continental writers."* He has only resorted to the armoury of the unbeliever and the sceptic in every age, and the weapons he has discovered there are by no means invincible.

I need scarcely remark, that it would not be possible, in these pages, to examine *seriatim*, all the difficulties advanced by Dr. Colenso. But I propose to point out the fallacy of *some* of them, and I pledge myself in my selection to have regard to the *principal* difficulties.

As I have just said, Dr. Colenso mainly occupies himself with a critical examination of the historical narrative of the Exodus, and his difficulties are almost entirely arithmetical. Incidentally, however, rather than of set purpose, he has alluded, in the preface of his work, to difficulties of a moral and scientific nature. Perhaps, therefore, a very brief reference to these may fitly precede the consideration of the arithmetical difficulties by which, more immediately, he attempts to prove that the narrative of the Exodus cannot be historically true.

* Preface. P. xiv

The MORAL difficulties relate to *Slavery* and the *Destruction of the Midianites.*

On the subject of *Slavery* Dr. Colenso quotes Exodus xxi., 4, and xxi., 20-21 :—

"If the master [of a Hebrew servant] have given him a wife, and she have borne him sons or daughters, the wife and her children shall be her master's, and he shall go out free by himself." Ex. xxi., 4.

"If a man smite his servant, or his maid, with a rod, and he die under his hand, he shall surely be punished. Notwithstanding, if he continue a day or two, he shall not be punished : for he is his money." Ex. xxi., 20-21.

Dr. Colenso writes:—"I shall never forget the revulsion of feeling, with which a very intelligent Zulu first heard these passages. His whole soul revolted against the notion, that the great and blessed God, the Father of all mankind, would speak of a servant or maid as mere 'money,' and allow a horrible crime to go unpunished, because the victim of his brutal usage had survived a few hours. My own heart and conscience at the time fully sympathised with his."*

In replying to this difficulty, I remark, in the first place, that Dr. Colenso has perverted the meaning of the passages quoted. As regards Ex. xxi., 4, he has forgotten, or omitted to cite, the following verses (5, 6,) which state that *it was optional* with the Hebrew slave whether he left his wife and children or not : if he preferred the latter he might remain with them in his master's house. As regards Ex. xxi., 21, 22, I deny altogether that it contains "the revolting notion" which Dr. Colenso sees in it. The reasonable interpretation may be thus given :—"If the servant died under the master's hand, although the master might plead that he was only using 'the rod' of correction, it was not to avail him anything : correction that could *possibly* issue in the *immediate death* of the servant, was unlawful correction, and, therefore, in the case of such death, the master was to be held guilty of the crime of murder ; the absolute law of life for life

* P. 9.

was to be vindicated, and the capital penalty inflicted." (Thus far the passage proves that the Hebrew slave had moral rights, and could not be reckoned merely as the " goods and chattels" of his owner.) " But, if the servant smitten should ' continue '—not ' a few hours ' as Dr. Colenso puts it—but ' a day or two,'— if life should be so far prolonged as to justify the conclusion that correction *only* was intended, then the master was *not* to be held guilty of murder. The words ' for he is his money,' so far from bearing the meaning Dr. Colenso assigns to them, namely, that God accounted the slave ' *mere* money,' were evidently added as *a reason for this conclusion :*—they simply recognise Slavery as an existing institution, and imply that no master would (unless actuated by a murderous intention) deprive himself of his servant who possessed to him a money value beyond his services."

The quotations thus understood, I remark, secondly, that the existence and regulation of Slavery amongst the Hebrews, was nothing more than *a permitted concession*, made in an age of iron, to " a stiff-necked people," lest worse should befal them, owing to the " hardness of their hearts." Had Dr. Colenso recognised this fact, he would have seen in the Mosaic law, which required the capital punishment of any master who by cruelty occasioned the death of a servant, a Divine provision *utterly opposed* to Slavery in its common form—a provision which most effectually guarded against the abuse of the concession made to the Hebrews, and prepared the people, as a nation, to receive, in a higher dispensation, the " New Commandment," with its added motives and sanctions, as the complete charter of human freedom. I say " with its added motives and sanctions :" for it must be remembered, the commandment was "new" *only* in this respect. The " second great commandment"—" Thou shalt love thy neighbour as thyself"—was as well known to the Jews as it is to us : Jesus quoted it from the Pentateuch, when He uttered those memorable words,—" On these two commandments hang all the Law and the Prophets." (Matt. xxii., 35, 40 ; Lev. xix., 18.)*

* An unaccountable ignorance of this *unity* of Jewish and Christian teaching in the enforcement of moral and spiritual obligations, prevails in many quarters. The writer recently received by post a Newspaper article—"Are we to be Jews or

I confess I could better have comprehended Dr. Colenso's "revulsion of feeling," if it had been directed against the existence of Slavery in *America:* and, in that case, so far from allowing that the books of Moses could be quoted in support of Slavery, I know not how the cause of Abolition could more effectively and *safely* be promoted, than by the enactment of *this very law* laid down in Exodus, the design of which has been so grievously misinterpreted. Were it once understood, in the Southern Slave States, that *the life of the master would be the penalty for the life of the slave*, not only would the horrors of slavery be greatly diminished, but "the axe would be laid at the very root of the tree." This recognition, however limited, of a slave's moral rights, would be found to be quite incompatible with the maintenance of slavery as an institution.*

Christians?"—in which Judaism is actually charged not only with the introduction of false views of God, but even with the encouragement of immoralities of conduct, which are said to prevail to an unknown extent amongst professing Christians. Dr. Colenso's book is hailed as the harbinger of true Christian light. "He has helped us to get rid of the Pentateuch, and now we shall begin to be Christians instead of Jews!" That this trash should be put into the hands of the working classes of the community by newspapers boasting of an almost incredible circulation is a most painful consideration. May it not account in a great measure for the alienation of so many of our working men from the Christian Church? Let Christian people strenuously exert themselves to displace this pernicious literature by promoting the circulation of such publications as "The British Workman," "The Happy Home," "The Christian World," "The Church of England Magazine, Meliora," "The Leisure Hour," "The Sunday at Home," "The Christian Treasury," "The Quiver," "The Family Treasury," "Good Words," "The British Mothers' Magazine," "The Christian News," "Parish Magazine," &c.

* A Reviewer observes:—"It is somewhat strange that Bishop Colenso who desired to tolerate polygamy in his diocese,"—[on the ground that "it is not sinful and wicked in itself, and contrary to *all* religion, though it is contrary to the spirit of Christianity,"]—"it is somewhat strange that the very man who thus, in Natal, tried to draw back from the purity of the Gospel into the allowed, conceded (not *approved*) license of Judaism, when he finds in the laws of Moses a modified tolerance of slavery, feels his moral sense is revolted! Let him pay a visit to Virginia or Louisiana, and he may find clergymen, and even bishops, who will be shocked at his lax ideas on the law of marriage, but who will stoutly maintain the excellence of the Mosaic slave laws. An impartial man will see in all that Moses did, a great advance in the right direction. The wife and the slave both received protection. The absolute power exercised over slaves, even in civilized nations like Greece and Rome, was taken away. The power of punishment was left—indeed, without it, slavery could scarcely exist; but it was limited, and man-stealing was made a capital offence. In lieu of indignantly complaining that the Mosaic code went no further than this, the

The moral difficulty which Dr. Colenso connects with the account of *the Destruction of the Midianites*, is a difficulty which might equally bo urged against *every* exhibition of the righteous judgment of God in the ordinary government of the world. Mr. Rogers has forcibly remarked, " The pestilence, the famine, the volcano, present phenomena in tho works and ways of God which are, to all appearance, no less opposed to our conceptions of equity and goodness, than these so-called ' difficulties of Scripture.' "* It becomes us to remember that " Secret things belong to God "—that our limited capacities are not equal to the task of " Finding out the Almighty to perfection." " The fly perched upon the dome of St. Paul's, and trying to make out the architect's design, is only a faint resemblance of a human being, striving to grasp, to understand, and to pass sentence upon, the justice and benevolence of God's government of the Universe." It is enough for us to know that " God is love," and that " The Judge of all the earth must do right." The Reviewer in the *Christian Observer*, gives this answer to Dr. Colenso :—

"Does Dr. Colenso believe that such a city as Jerusalem ever existed ? Does he believe that it was destroyed by Titus ? Does he believe that *eleven hundred thousand* persons, men, women, and children, perished in this siege, by the most horrible modes of destruction, and that all the survivors were sold into hopeless slavery ?"

"Further : Does he not know, that this dreadful visitation was foreseen and foretold by Him who was the Divine personification of unspeakable love ? Does he not know that Jesus, foreseeing all this, could weep over the devoted city, but could not, or would not, spare it ? Does he doubt that all this vast and immeasurable amount of human suffering and wretchedness was ordained of God, and executed by His special permission ?"

"If he does not believe all this, we should deem it a waste of time to argue with him. But if he is not sceptical touching the deeds of Vespasian and Titus, we should like to know what he

bishop would have done more wisely to have compared the laws of Moses with those of other nations of ancient days, and to have acknowledged the important improvement."—*Christian Observer*.

* Defence of the Eclipse of Faith. P. 42.

gains by disbelieving the books of Moses. If I believe that God showed himself a God of vengeance in the greater case, what do I gain by rejecting the thought in the smaller?"*

The SCIENTIFIC difficulties to which Dr. Colenso also makes a passing allusion, are *Geological* and *Astronomical.*

Without discussing supposed *Geological difficulties,* we may fairly ask the question—If Geology is really opposed to the Bible, how is it that such men as Owen, and Sedgwick, and Anderson, and Hitchcock, and Buckland, and Chalmers, and Miller, and Pye Smith, have never found it out, but retain and assert their profound reverence for the Scriptures? We do not say that the opening chapters of Genesis were designed to furnish us with a cosmogony. The discoveries of science were not anticipated or forestalled. But we believe that scientific discoveries can never *contradict* the Bible, and we have confidence in the testimony of such men as Hugh Miller, who declared—" I know not a single scientific truth that militates against even the minutest or least prominent of the details of Genesis." Although the Bible is admittedly not a book of science, men of science owe a debt to it—a debt which might be fairly estimated by comparing the Mosaic account of the Creation with the conceptions of the wisest philosophers who possessed *only* the light of philosophy to guide them. " Without the Mosaic history the world would be in total darkness, not knowing whence it came, or whither it goeth. In the first page of this Sacred Book a child may learn more in an hour, than all the philosophers in the world learned without it in thousands of years." With special reference to this point, it has been asked with irresistible force,—" Does it not in truth involve a far higher difficulty, to suppose that the writer of the book of Genesis, without Divine enlightenment, rose so far above his age as to invent the account of the creation, which he is hinted to have palmed upon mankind as a revelation, than to suppose that higher discoveries of science will manifest to all the essential truth-fulness of that account?"†

The chief *Astronomical difficulty* is that of " the sun standing still at the word of Joshua." Of course the language used in describing this miracle is language adapted to the common and popular phraseology. Scientific men still speak, even in scientific works, of " the sun *rising* " and " the sun *setting*." Literally this is incorrect, but all understand it. Of the miracle itself it would suffice to say, He who called the sun and moon into existence is not to be limited in the exercise of His power. But the following comment may be satisfactory to some minds. " As there is at all times in God's works what may be termed ' the economy of power,' which economy is the necessary result of perfect wisdom, it is possible that the continuation of day, which was the object to be obtained, might have been effected by a miracle in another form to what is commonly understood—that is, *by a prolonged refraction of the rays of light*. To strengthen this supposition, an eminent scholar maintains that the words in the original, expressive of the sun and moon, are not the words which generally denote those bodies, but words that denote rather the solar and the lunar light."*

I proceed now to the consideration of the principal difficulties urged by Dr. Colenso, in the volume he has written, bearing more immediately upon the question of THE HISTORICAL VERACITY OF THE PENTATEUCH. It will be remembered that he alleges that these present " a series of manifest, absolute, palpable self-contradictions, inconsistencies, and impossibilities." How far his allegation, so strongly and decidedly expressed, is established, we shall soon be able to determine.

I.—The first difficulty, with which Dr. Colenso opens his attack, turns upon this verse in the account of the migration of Jacob's family into Egypt :—

"And the sons of Judah, Er, and Onan, and Shelah, and Pharez, and Zarah ; but Er and Onan died in the land of Canaan ; and the sons of Pharez, Hezron, and Hamul." (Gen. xlvi., 12.)

He sets to work to prove that Hezron and Hamul could not have been born at the time of the migration ; and hence, that the whole narrative is untrue, and unhistorical, since their names are given in this list of those who went down into Egypt.

His difficulty may be met in two ways. It may be met, first, by the simple reply, that the Bible does not say that Hezron and Hamul *were* born at the time of the migration. Strangely enough, Dr. Colenso's first quotation from Scripture is a *mis*quotation. He omits the word "were" in the last clause : "And the sons of Pharez *were* Hezron and Hamul." It is evident that the Inspired writer first sets down all Judah's sons; and then adds two after-thoughts, to make it quite clear *what* members of Jacob's family went down in Egypt : 1. That Er and Onan had died in Canaan ; 2. That Pharez had two sons *who were reckoned* as filling their places, whether born in Canaan or Egypt. Another answer which has been given equally meets the difficulty, namely, that although the Bible does not say that Hezron and Hamul *were* born at the time of the migration, they *may* have been. "In Genesis xxvi., 34, we learn that Esau (twin with Jacob) was forty years old when he married. This gave Rebekah the excuse for sending Jacob away. (Gen. xxvii., 46.) Hence, if he reached Laban's house in his forty-first year, and was married to Leah and Rachel in his forty-eighth, there would remain a period of more than eighty years before his going down to Egypt, when he was 130 years of age. (Gen. xlviii., 9.) In this interim, there was abundance of time for Judah's birth and marriage, the death of Er and Onan, the birth of Pharez, and his marriage, and the birth of Hezron and Hamul. It is extraordinary that this very obvious solution should never have occurred to Bishop Colenso ; but we cannot see that he even alludes to it." *

It thus appears that this first difficulty is entirely of Dr. Colenso's own making : and that, even if it did exist, an explanation of it may be given which is far more tenable than his own view of the history.

Since this difficulty is a specimen of others of a similar kind, it may be well to observe, that the orthodox view of Inspiration embracing both the Divine and human element, by no means

* *Christian Observer.* Dec., p. 926, 927.

implies that the Holy Spirit inspired men in the knowledge of the commonest facts, or of things which passed under their own observation. We plead only for " such a complete and immediate communication by the Holy Spirit to the minds of the sacred writers, of *those things which could not otherwise have been known;* and such an effectual superintendency, as to those particulars concerning which they might otherwise obtain information, as sufficed absolutely to preserve them from every degree of error in all things which could in the least degree affect any of the doctrines or precepts contained in their writings."* When, therefore, we meet with genealogies and family lists such as this, the most rational supposition is, that they were copied from the public records extant at the time : and then, unless we can prove that the Divine purpose in their insertion *required* infallible correctness, any trifling imperfections would be rightly traced to the " human element" in Scripture, without detracting *one iota* from the Divine. Unquestionably the Bible does contain *some* such imperfections, but they are in every instance unimportant and immaterial—as unimportant as the question whether Hezron and Hamul were born before the migration into Egypt, or a few years later.

II.—After this weak and futile commencement, Dr. Colenso plunges into his own peculiar element, and favours us with what the Athenæum describes as " Colenso's Arithmetic applied to the Bible."

Before I proceed to notice a few of these arithmetical puzzles, I would make the general remark applicable to them all—*that they rest on a very uncertain basis.* It is well known that errors in numbers are common in all ancient works, and we admit they are to be found in the Bible. For instance we read in 1 Sam. vi., 19, that the Lord smote of the people of Bethshemeth, a small town, "Fifty thousand and three score and ten men ;" and in Jud. xii., 6, we read, that " There fell at the passage of the Jordan, of the Ephraimites forty and two thousand." These numbers are incredibly large. But, as it happens, we are easily able to

* *Rev. Thomas Scott's Commentary.*

correct the manifest errors, by understanding the idiom of the language—an idiom still in use among the Arabs. They say in the year 12 and 300 for 312. Hence, 1 Sam. vi., 19, literally translated, reads—the Lord smote "seventy men, fifties, and a thousand;" or 1,170, not 50,070:—and Jud. xii., 6, reads, "There fell of the Ephraimites forty, and two thousand;" or, 2,040, not 42,000. Another example occurs in 2 Chron. vii., 5, "Twenty-two thousand," should be 20 and 2,000, or 2,020.* Dr. Colenso himself remarks—"It is impossible for us not to perceive that a systematic habit of exaggeration in respect to numbers prevails among Hebrew writers of history, probably from not realising to their own minds the actual meaning and magnitude of the numbers employed."† I should rather attribute this apparent exaggeration to our ignorance of prevailing idioms. May there not be a *truthful* use of the figure hyperbole, in its application to numbers, as we apply it in general terms? At any rate, we may rest assured that the numbers were accurately understood by the Jews.

Whether, then, we are able to solve all Dr. Colenso's arithmetical puzzles or no, they can never shake our confidence in the historical veracity of the Old Testament. The Rev. S. Prideaux Tregelles well observes:—"In criticism it holds good as a sound canon, that difficulties connected with dates and numbers, are not in themselves legitimate grounds for rejecting any document; because translators of numbers (just like modern compositors with regard to figures), were more habitually liable to err in these things than in anything else." There is certainly no reason why we should make the credibility of the Pentateuch depend on the accuracy of numbers, as we find them in our *present* Hebrew text.

At the same time it must not be supposed that Dr. Colenso has really alleged numeral difficulties that are *insuperable*. Even allowing the number of the Children of Israel to be as high as he states it, we are by no means at a loss to disprove the so-called "impossibilities" which he connects with this number. This disproof it will now be our aim to furnish.

* Taylor, in Calmet.   † P. 142.

III. One of Dr. Colenso's numerical " impossibilities " is this. He finds repeated commands in Exodus and Numbers that " all the congregation" shall appear before " the door of the Tabernacle" or " before the Lord ;" and he reads that " Moses and Joshua addressed all Israel." He measures the tabernacle, and he estimates the power of the human voice ; and he pronounces the words " impossible !"—" inconceivable !"*

A Reviewer comments on this objection with an allowable degree of severity : " Not more ' inconceivable,' than that a grown man, who has hitherto been supposed to have an average knowledge of ordinary affairs, should complacently print and publish such trash as this ! Where can this writer have been living, that he should be so entirely in the dark as to the commonest usages of mankind ? Matthew of Westminster tells us, that in A.D. 1297, the king, being involved in two wars and finding it necessary to lay heavy burdens on the people, summoned the people of London to meet him at Westminster Hall, when he addressed them and explained his position. Bishop Colenso might take out his pencil, demonstrate that 50,000 or 100,000 people could not stand in, or in front of Westminster Hall, and that the king's voice could not reach them, and so prove—to his own satisfaction —that the story was ' inconceivable,' and that Matthew's Chronicle was ' unhistorical,' i. e. untrue ! But all common-place people could tell the bishop that such things occur in common life every year ; that 20,000 men are frequently summoned to meet in Guildhall which could not admit one quarter of them. To urge objections of this kind against the Pentateuch is the very wanton-ness of scepticism." †

IV. Dr. Colenso next objects, that the adult male descendants of the sixty-six members of Jacob's family, who went down with him into Egypt, could not have reached the number of 600,000 at the Exodus.

We reply—the Bible does not say they did. Dr. Colenso " assumes, that it is absolutely undeniable, that the narrative of the Exodus distinctly involves the statement, that the 66 persons mentioned in Gen. xlvi., and *no others*, went down with him into Egypt."* But this is *bare* assumption. The very texts which he quotes to support it seem to prove the contrary. The writer of the Inspired narrative is careful to inform us, that "all the souls of the *house* of Jacob"—"the *children* of Israel"—"that came out of the loins of Jacob" (Gen. xlvi., 26, 27. Ex. i., 1, 5)— were 66 ; but this very care implies that he is distinguishing the family of Jacob from *the dependants who accompanied them.* Abraham had 318 such dependants 200 years before, and there is every reason to believe, that the whole *household* of Jacob who came with him into Egypt, amounted to at least 500 persons of both sexes. The supposed difficulty at once vanishes.

V. The march out of Egypt, the possession of arms, and the supply of tents, are fresh difficulties to Dr. Colenso.

The movements of so large a body of people seem incredible to him. We may remind him, that Herodotus records the march and passage across the Hellespont of the army of Xerxes, numbering 1,700,000 foot, and 80,000 horse. Bishop Thirlwall remarks— "There seems no sufficient ground for supposing that these estimates are greatly exaggerated." Would Dr. Colenso conclude, because of the number of Xerxes's army, that Herodotus has palmed fiction upon us in the place of history ?

But Dr. Colenso continues—"The Israelites were furnished with tents—how could they carry them ? They were all armed, and where did they get their arms ?" We reply,—when they spoiled the Egyptians they most likely took whatever was most urgently needed for their flight. Some cover for the night would be indispensable, and this they would contrive in some way. " Dr. Colenso talks of poles and cords as if the tents had come from Edgington's." It is not probable that they had anything like our *modern* tents, but whatever they had to cover them and theirs, however temporary, slight, and untentlike, it was a tent for all practical purposes. Most travellers in the East could inform Dr. Colenso, that to this day, the common Arab tent, for a whole family, consists of little more than a long shawl, stretched over a few sticks.

As to the Israelites being armed, we are not to infer that every man had his sword, and shield, and javelin. The word which Dr. Colenso renders " armed," is in our translation " harnessed." It is a word of most doubtful etymology., Gesenius says it may mean " eager," " brave," " prepared for battle." According to the Septuagint, it denotes that the people went out in orderly *ranks of five or fifty.* But " harnessed," in the sense of " equipped," is the better rendering, and would of course involve no difficulty. The fugitives carried their kneading troughs, clothes (part of their equipment), &c., on their shoulders, and doubtless many of them were partially armed, either with weapons brought from Egypt, or obtained, as Josephus records, from the slain Egyptians at the Red Sea.

VI.—The extent of the camp compared with the priest's duties : the celebration of the Passover : the supply of lambs and pigeons for sacrifice : furnish another set of objections.

For the most part these objections are based upon the assumption, that the whole Levitical sacrificial system was in full operation in the wilderness. The Review of Dr. Colenso's work in the *Morning Post*, contains some admirable remarks on this point :—

" We must here express our surprise that a man so accustomed to mathematical reasoning as Dr. Colenso is, should not have seen that there is a most important link wanting in his chain, viz., that it is anywhere said that the whole of this burdensome ceremonial was to be observed in the wilderness. The laws given by Moses were for all time till Christ should come, and they were delivered at intervals in the journey to the land of promise. The period of the Jewish wanderings was the period of their instruction in the principles of religion, government, and civil society. Moses, whose authority was supreme, was not only their deliverer, but their historian, lawgiver, and prophet. He was not to enter the promised land, but to die on the other side of Jordan. It was necessary, not only for the training of the people, but for the fulfilment of his own mission, that the whole ecclesiastical and municipal code should be delivered before his death, and before the Israelites passed over Jordan. But it is not to be therefore assumed that the whole ceremonial, with all its burdensome difficulty—ordained for permanent observance—was to come into instant operation in the midst of the still more burdensome and exceptional state of things that prevailed in the wilderness. That this is clear appears from the internal evidence. Take, for example, the directions about leprosy in houses, the instructions to scrape the walls and purify the foundations. Could this apply to the tents in the desert? Take, again, the allusion to houses and walled cities in this very ceremonial law, and to fields and vineyards. There were none of these in the wilderness. More especially ought the recurrence of such passages as these to be deemed conclusive —'And it shall be when the **lord** thy God shall bring thee into the land of the Canaanites, as He sware unto thee and to thy fathers, and shall give it thee, then thou shalt set apart unto the Lord, &c. &c.' (Exod. xiii., 11) ; and notably in Deut. iv., 14—'And the Lord commanded me at that time to teach you statutes and judgments, that ye might do them in the land whither ye go over to possess it.' We conceive that there can be no doubt in any candid mind that the operation of the greater part of the Jewish law was prospective, and was not in force during the journey to Canaan. And if so, Dr. Colenso's mountain about the impossibility of Aaron, Eleazar, and Ithamar being able, in the simple particulars of time and physical strength, to offer up all the burnt-offerings, meat-offerings, peace-offerings, sin-offerings, trespass-offerings, thank-offerings for a population like that of London, and all the hitch about the need of 500 pigeons per diem, becomes a very insignificant molehill which a small amount of reasonable faith may suffice to cast into the sea."

In dealing with this part of his subject, the blind determination of Dr. Colenso to see nothing but difficulties, is most remarkable. He can make no allowance for any possible departure from the literal and full discharge of the Levitical ceremonial law. For instance, he finds a merciful provision allowing the offering of " turtle doves or young pigeons," whenever the lamb would be beyond the means of the offerer. It only suggests to him a fresh objection :—" Where could the people find turtle doves and young pigeons in the wilderness ?" He adds, with irreverent sarcasm,—" Did the people carry *these* with them out of Egypt ?"* But presently he answers his own objection. He admits that the Hebrew word, translated " pigeon," may be translated " bird of the wilderness," and confirms his admission by quotations from other parts of the Bible ; (Ps. lv., 6-7, Jer. xlviii., 28, Eze. vii., 16.) It is true, he tries to destroy the force of this admission, by arguing that the wilderness spoken of in these passages was not like the wilderness of Sinai. It was only " an uncultivated and *comparatively* barren country : "—in the wilderness of *Sinai* even " birds of the wilderness could not be found ! " But once more he stultifies his own argument by

* Dr. Colenso, p. 124.

confessing, in the same paragraph, that the Hebrew word for "wilderness" is the *same* in every passage.*

With regard to the celebration of the Passover, the remarks of KURTZ are worthy of consideration. He says—" We are brought to the conclusion that the Mosaic Law permitted the lambs to be killed in private houses, provided the houses were within the camp or city, in which the Tabernacle was erected : and that the priestly vocation of the Israelites as a body, (Ex. xix., 6)—not suspended when the Passover was first instituted, (Ex xx., 19)—enabled them to supplement the special offices discharged by Aaron and his sons in these particulars." Even Dr. Colenso admits—" It is certainly true that the references to the Passover, in the books of Exodus and Numbers, do not appear to imply in any way that the priests were called into action in the celebration of this feast." He *ought* to have said " *such* action" as to give any countenance to the objection raised on the ground of the multiplicity of their duties. †

* "Bishop Colenso marvels where the Hebrew women got ninety thousand pigeons annually for sacrifice. There is no marvel in the case : the pigeons were not obtained. We learn from Lev. xii., 3-8, that the sacrifices were to be offered after the rite of circumcision; but Josh. v., 5-7, shows that circumcision was not practised in the wilderness : we therefore see that the pigeons would not be required."—*The Quiver.*

† "Bishop Colenso says there were but three priests in the wilderness, and they could not have offered all the sacrifices required. Without entering into calculations as to the number of sacrifices required, because no man can say how many were offered in the wilderness, we may readily admit that three priests could not have offered them all. But were there *only three priests ?* Beyond all question, Aaron and his two sons, Eleazar and Ithamar, were the priests in a strict and special sense. Nor do we doubt that their labours were very heavy ; so heavy were they indeed, that Korah, Dathan, and Abiram said to them, as well as to Moses, " Ye take too much upon you." This is what Dr. Colenso says they did. But is it reasonable to imagine that these three priests did not employ the thousands of Levites about them, in all holy duties possible ? The passages quoted by the bishop against this view, have nothing to do with the case. Until he can prove that the Levites were called "strangers," (Num. iii., 10, 38) the texts he quotes will rather make for our opinion. The word rendered " stranger " means any layman or ordinary person, and not a Levite. We conclude, then, that Aaron and his fellow-priests employed the Levites to assist them as much as they thought proper. We do *not* find that Aaron and his own sons had no assistants, but we *do* find that the tribe of Levi was wholly set apart for sacred functions. The duties of Eleazar, in particular, are specified in Num. iii., 16, and this is, after all, the best answer to our objector, especially if taken in connection with such texts as Num. xvi., 8, 9. The truth is, that Aaron and his own sons

In the same narrow spirit Dr. Colenso quotes the command in
Lev. iv., 11, 12, that "The priest shall carry forth without the
camp the carcase of the sin-offering," and understands by it, that
"Aaron himself, or one of his sons, would have had to carry the
carcase on his back, on foot, a distance of six miles." He adds,
"The supposition involves an absurdity: but it is our duty to
look plain facts in the face."* The absurdity rests with Dr. Colenso,
who ought to have known enough of Hebrew, and of English too,
to comprehend that a man is often said to do himself what he does
by or *through* another. It is obvious that the priest *caused* the
carcase to be conveyed from the altar in front of the Tabernacle to
be burnt in some convenient place: and there appears to have been
"waggons" for this very purpose, which had been offered to the
Levites long before, at the dedication of the Tabernacle. The
assumed distance of "six miles" is equally imaginary. We know
of no proof that the expression, "without the camp," necessarily
means, "beyond the extreme lines of the whole encampment of
the Israelites." Each tribe had a separate camp, and the spaces
between the camps might be considered "without the camp:" so
that the distance would be comparatively short.

VII.—The maintenance of the sheep and cattle of the Israelites
in the desert, is another of Dr. Colenso's "impossibilities." He
argues that it is incredible that such vast flocks as the Israelites
must have possessed in order to furnish the legal sacrifices, could
have found food and water in the wilderness.

The fact of an *allowed limitation* in the observance of the
Levitical law, of course robs this objection of half its
force. The remaining half is not very formidable. Dr.
Colenso labours hard to prove, that there could not be
sufficient herbage in the wilderness: and even ventures to
say, that "The water from the rock did *not* follow the people as

---

were *chief priests*, and were responsible for the right performance of what was
done under their direction. What was so done, was regarded as done by them.
Thus Solomon is said to have built the Temple (1 Kings vi., 14); Jacob carried
away all his cattle and goods (Gen. xxxi., 18); and Nebuchadnezzar carried away
all Jerusalem (2 Kings xxiv., 14).—*The Quiver.*

* P. 40.

some have supposed."* He makes another glaring *mis*quotation to prove this : " Beware that thou forget not Jehovah thy God, who led thee through that great and terrible wilderness, wherein were fiery serpents, and scorpions, and drought, *where there was no water ;*"—Here he stops,—whereas the very next words assert the fact which the bishop denies :—" *Who brought thee forth water out of the rock of flint.*" (Deut. viii., 11, 15.) Doubtless the quotation was taken second-hand and never verified : but what an illustration have we here of the carelessness with which this matter has been examined, and of " the deep-seated and fore-gone prejudice which has left its indelible brand upon every page of the book." † As to the supply of herbage, we are little able to form a judgment. The Author of " Sinai and Palestine," Dr. Stanley, points out natural remains, which prove that a far more abundant vegetation must have formerly existed. Dr. Colenso strongly insists upon the absolute literality of Deut. xxxii., 10, as descriptive of the wilderness, but who does not know that the figure hyperbole is naturally used in speaking of afflictive circumstances, even as it is easily understood ?

Moreover, it seems that, during by far the greater part of the period of forty years, [36 years,] the Israelites lived near the populous Mount Seir and the Red Sea, where they could not fail to come into commercial intercourse with rich nations and tribes, who would provide them with the necessaries of life in exchange for the gold and silver and other precious property which they possessed. (Deut. ii., 6.) Dr. Colenso, indeed, tells us, that " the Scripture story says not a word about this long sojourn." Yet, in the very same page,‡ he quotes Deut. ii., 1, " We compassed Mount Seir *many days,*"—an expression which, according to the Hebrew idiom, is significant of an indefinite time.

We have now gone through the principal objections which Dr. Colenso has urged against THE HISTORICAL VERACITY OF THE PENTATEUCH. Although our refutation has been brief, it will, I think, suffice to satisfy us, that so far from these objections pro-

---

* Pp. 66, 67.   † *Record.*   ‡ P. 76.

senting " a series of manifest, absolute, palpable self-contradictions, inconsistencies and impossibilities," we have nothing whatever to fear from the bishop's assault upon Bible Inspiration. The
volume he has so hastily written, has been fitly described, by one
of its ablest Reviewers, as " The most narrow-minded book that
has been published since the rise of Rationalism among English
divines."* Even the *Saturday Review*, with all its latitudinarian
sympathies, expresses this decided judgment :—" Some of Dr.
Colenso's difficulties are undoubtedly hypercritical ; some
frivolous and almost puerile ; whilst others, (as for instance that
regarding the alleged want of preparation for the Passover,) seem
to rest upon misconception, or even careless oversight; and it
must be added, that, so lax and reckless is the character of the
objector's mind, in several places he even copies incorrectly the
very passages on which he founds his arguments." " Singularly,
indeed, must that mind be constituted, which could balance such
imaginary difficulties against the solid and coherent Evidences of
the Faith. We believe, that, never in the history of controversy
have such strong conclusions been rested on such feeble proofs :
it is like balancing a mountain upon a pin's point. The book
demonstrates in its author either the haste of ignorance or the
blindness of prejudice."†

I dismiss our second topic with a quotation from the pen of
Professor Rawlinson, a scholar of European reputation, in which
he gives the result of his learned investigations. He says :—

"It appears, then, from this whole review, that there is nothing in the history
of the world, so far as it is yet known, that forms even a serious objection to the
authenticity of the Pentateuch.".....,"The more accurately old myths are
examined, the more evident does it become that their tone and spirit are
wholly different from the tone and spirit of Scripture. The Pentateuch has the
air and manner of history; the Jews have always regarded it in that light; and
modern historical and geographical inquiries, whenever they afford an oppor-
tunity of testing the accuracy of the narrative, are found to bear witness to its
truth. Whatever may be the scientific difficulties in the way of a literal recep-
tion of some portions, historical difficulties of any real magnitude there are none.
Internally, the narrative is consistent with itself: externally, it is supported by
all that has any claim to be considered sober earnest in the histories of other
nations. The Christian world, which has reposed upon it for nearly 2,000 years,
as an authentic record of the earliest ages, is justified by all the results of

modern historical research, in still continuing its confident trust. There is really not a pretence for saying that recent discoveries in the field of history, monumental or other, have made the acceptance of the Mosaic narrative in its plain and literal sense any more difficult now than in the days of Bossuet or Stillingfleet."

III.

Our Lord's Conclusive Testimony to the Inspiration of the Pentateuch.

The treatment of our third topic must be compressed within narrow limits, but its importance cannot possibly be over-estimated. It is the very pivot on which the whole controversy between Dr. Colenso and believers in Bible Inspiration, turns. It brings to bear upon the question at issue the solemn fact, *that our blessed Lord, in the most positive manner, bound up His own credibility with the historical reality of Moses and the Inspired character of his writings.*

We say that CHRIST PLEDGED HIMSELF TO THE VERACITY OF THE OLD TESTAMENT SCRIPTURES. The authority of the Old Testament, and the authority of Christ, must therefore stand, or fall together. In proportion as the authority of the Old Testament is weakened, our Lord, who is ever appealing to it, and quoting from it, is discredited.

I can only present a very brief summary of the *chief* passages, in which our Lord's conclusive testimony is given to the Inspiration of the Old Testament—and the Pentateuch as an integral portion of it.* Mr. Birk's Volume, " The Bible and Modern

---

* A correspondent of the *Record* gives the following selection of quotations from the four Gospels, exhibiting our Lord's testimony to the PENTATEUCH only :—

The Institution and Law of Marriage : Matt. xix., 3-8. Comp. Gen. ii., 24.

The Flood : Matt. xxiv., 37-39. Luke xvii., 26, 27. Comp. Gen. vi.-viii.

The Wickedness and Destruction of the Cities of the Plain : Luke xvii., 28-32. Matt. x., 14, 15 ; xi., 23, 24. Comp. Gen. xix.

The Institution of Circumcision : John vii., 22. Comp. Gen. xvii., 10-14.

The Revelation at the Burning Bush : Matt. xxii., 29-32 ; Mark xii., 26, 27 ; Luke xx., 37, 38. Comp. Ex. iii.

The Passover : Matt. xxvi., 18-20 ; John xix., 36 ; John i., 29. Comp. Ex. xii.

Thought," contains a chapter on the subject which, if it could be bound up with every copy of Dr. Colenso's book, would effectually counteract its influence for evil. I shall simply establish by quotations the following points ;—*Christ's fulfilment of the Scriptures;* —and *Christ's recognition of the sovereign authority of the Scriptures.*

I.—CHRIST'S FULFILMENT OF THE SCRIPTURES.

The Old Testament declares what Jesus Christ would *be,* and *do,* and *suffer*: all of which He was, and did, and suffered. In the Gospels we constantly read, this and that was done, " that it might be fulfilled which was spoken by the prophet." Christ's own attestation to this fulfilment of the Scriptures, is again and again given.

"Think not that I am come to destroy the Law, or the Prophets: I am not come to destroy, but to fulfil. For verily I say unto you, Till heaven and earth pass, one jot or one tittle shall in no wise pass from the law, till all be fulfilled." (Matt. v., 17, 18.)

"And He began to say unto them, This day is this Scripture fulfilled in your ears." (Luke iv., 16, 21.)

"Had ye believed Moses, ye would have believed Me : for he wrote of Me." (John v., 46.)

"For I say unto you, that this that is written must yet be accomplished in Me, And He was reckoned among the transgressors : for the things concerning Me have an end." (Luke xxii., 37.)

"And He said unto them, These are the words which I spake unto you, while I was yet with you, that all things must be fulfilled, which were written in the Law of Moses, and in the Prophets, and in the Psalms, concerning Me." (Luke xxiv., 44.)

The Law of the Ten Commandments: Matt. xix., 16, 19; xv., 3-6; xxii., 35-40; Mark vii., 9-13. Comp. Ex. xx.

The Mosaic Law in General: Luke xxiv., 25-47; Matt. v., 17-19; Luke xvi., 31; John v., 45-47; John vii., 19.

Ceremonial Ordinances: Matt. viii., 2-4; Mark i., 44; Luke ii., 21-24. Comp. Lev. xii. and xiv.

The Brazen Serpent: John iii., 14, 15. Comp. Num. xxv.

Mosaic Precepts: Matt. iv., 4, 7, 10. Comp. Deut. viii., 3; vi., 16; and x., 20.

See also, Matt. viii., 17 ; xii., 16-19 ; xiii, 34, 85 ; xxi., 1-9 ; John v., 39.

II.—Christ's Recognition of the Sovereign Authority of the Scriptures.

"The only man ever capable of judging infallibly for Himself, was the man Christ Jesus : since right and wrong are what He knows and declares them to be : yet, He never did judge for Himself, but submitted His judgment to the written Word. He whose Spirit animated all the prophets of the Old Testament, (1 Pet. i, 11) knew ' The Scriptures could not be broken.' (John x., 35.)"*

With the Scriptures,—not with argument,—He met Satan in the wilderness. He repelled his thrice repeated attack with, " It is written ;" and each time He drew His arrow from the book of Deuteronomy. (Matt. iv., 1-11, comp. with Deut. viii., 3, vi., 16, 13.) One sentence of the Law of Moses,—one word from a Book which modern wisdom would regard as a compilation of myths and fiction,—outweighed, in Christ's judgment, all other considerations. And what is worthy of remark, Satan, the great Adversary, was compelled to yield to the authority of these quotations from the Pentateuch.

With the Scriptures He met the cavils of the Sadducees about the Resurrection, quoting Exodus iii., 6, " As touching the resurrection of the dead, have ye not read that which was *spoken unto you* by God, saying, I *am* the God of Abraham, and the God of Isaac, and the God of Jacob ? God is not the God of the dead, but of the living :" (Matt. xxii., 31-32)—the force of the quotation in this instance depending upon *verbal* accuracy—I *am*, &c.

With the Scriptures, He established His own Divine mission and authority (Matt. xxi., 13) ; confirmed His teaching (Luke vi., 1-5) ; and settled difficult questions, (Matt. xix., 3-6). In this *last* passage, the Mosaic account of the Creation and the Institution and Law of Marriage, is confirmed,—" Have ye not

---

* "The Scripture cannot be broken." An admirable Tract by the Rev. J. W. Reeve.

read, *that He which made them at the beginning* made them male
and female, and *said,"*—*i.e.* GOD SAID—" For this cause shall a man
leave father and mother, and shall cleave to his wife : and they
twain shall be one flesh. *What therefore God hath joined together,*
let no man put asunder :" (compare with Gen. i., 27, ii., 24.) In
the parallel passage in Mark x. our Lord puts the question,
" What did *Moses* command you ?"—the command of Moses being
regarded as equivalent to the command of GOD.

With the Scriptures He nerved Himself for suffering, (Luke
xviii., 31) and consoled Himself in His trials. (Mark xiv., 27.)
In the hour of His sorest conflict and deepest sorrow, His reverence for the authority of Scripture was more to Him than the
ministry of angelic aid : " Thinkest thou that I cannot now pray
to my Father, and He shall presently give me more than twelve
legions of angels ? *But how then shall the Scriptures be fulfilled,
that thus it must be.*" (Matt. xxvi., 53, 54.)

With the Scriptures, after His resurrection He taught the
disciples : "Beginning at Moses and all the prophets, He expounded
unto them in *all* the Scriptures, the things, (not the *myths* but the
' things,') " concerning Himself :"—(Luke xxiv., 25-27), and
His last act, before His ascension into Heaven, was to " open
their understanding, that they might understand the Scriptures."
(Luke xxiv. 45.)

Thus, then, the Great Teacher, Himself ESSENTIAL TRUTH,
affirmed, in the clearest and most positive language, THE DIVINE
AUTHORITY AND INSPIRATION OF THE SCRIPTURES OF THE OLD
TESTAMENT. He always recognised those Scriptures as the
" Oracles of God,"—the " utterances of God," deposited in a
written form by " holy men " who " spake " these utterances and
recorded them, " as they were moved by the Holy Ghost." (2
Pet. i., 21.) Again and again He endorsed their authority, and
asserted the perfection of the canon. Whilst He frequently charged
the Jews with " making the Word of God of none effect by their
traditions," He *never* accused them of corrupting the text, leaving
us to infer, that whatever flaws, contracted in the transmission of
the text, may be detected here and there by a strong microscope

of minute criticism, they are so few and slight, that for every
practical purpose they disappear from view. In hundreds of
quotations, bearing on the most vital points of doctrine, and on the
most weighty facts of Old Testament history, our Lord never found
it needful to allude to their existence, or to utter one caution
against undue confidence in the sacred text. As we have seen,—
" What saith the Scripture?" was His constant test of truth :—" It
is written," His invincible sword and shield under temptation :—
" The Scripture cannot be broken," His unvarying assertion of
their Divine immutability. And, as He leaves the world, He
gives to His Church one final testimony—explicit, full, conclusive,—
to the Divine Inspiration of all the Scriptures ; recognising
distinctly " the law of Moses, the Prophets, and the Psalms,"
(the well-known three-fold division of the Old Testament,) as the
vehicles of Divine prophecy respecting Himself, His sufferings,
His death, His resurrection, and His preached Gospel.

On Christ's Word of Testimony the Divine origin of the Old
Testament is established. Not, mark, the Divine origin of one
portion of the Book—of a division here and a text there, to be
selected according to the judgment of the so-called "verifying
faculty" in man,—but of the WHOLE. The Book is from beginning
to end pervaded with a Divine element. " All Scripture is
given by Inspiration of God." (2 Tim. iii., 16.)

We ask :—Can a contrast be conceived, more complete, than
that which exists between the Saviour, " opening and alleging out
of all the Scriptures the things concerning Himself," and the
unbelieving, flippant criticisms of men " wise in their own
conceits," falsifying the plainest records of the most certain facts ?
They " err not knowing the Scriptures." (Matt. xxii., 29.) Let
our prayer for them be—" Lord ! open thou their understanding,
that they may understand the Scriptures ! "

But, it will be asked,—Does not Dr. Colenso, in some way or
other, endeavour to parry the force of the conclusion so plainly
drawn from our Lord's testimony to the Old Testament Scriptures ?
He cannot be unconscious of the difficulty of his position,—how
does he propose to escape from the difficulty ?

The answer we must give to this question, is indeed a grave one. It will sadly prove to us that Dr. Colenso, unless arrested in his course, is nearing the precipice of final unbelief in the Divine authority of the Founder of Christianity. He absolutely adopts the conclusion that Christ was *ignorant* of the truth which he— Dr. Colenso—has discovered : in a word—*he is wiser than his Lord and Master!*

Dr. Colenso devotes but *one* page* to the consideration of this all-absorbing point—this pivot on which the whole controversy turns : and he tells us, in effect, that Christ was *mistaken*. "He could not be expected to speak of the Pentateuch in other terms than any other devout Jew of that day would have employed." The bishop, having brought himself to believe what to us is utterly incredible†—that the Jews had allowed myths, and contradictions, and impossibilities, involving the establishment of positive, outward, national institutions,—the Sabbath, Circumcision, the Passover,—to be palmed upon them as veritable history, Divinely recorded by Inspired men,—takes but one further step, and he believes—(miracle of incredulity!) that our blessed Lord, in utter ignorance, based his teaching upon a book of fictions, claiming in the name of God, the authority of facts! Such is the marvellous credulity of scepticism. In these modern days, we are to suppose that educated men—scholars with "advanced intellects" —"the more thoughtful portion of the community"‡—have a larger knowledge of the laws of historical criticism, the mysteries of science,—especially, we presume, of the science of *numbers*— than He who was Himself emphatically the Truth!

Dr. Colenso urges, in support of this monstrous theory, that Christ was *man*, and that "as man, He voluntarily entered into all the conditions of humanity, and among others, into that which makes our growth in all ordinary knowledge *gradual* and *limited*." Truly the bishops' ingenuity is great. We are reminded of a like ingenious attempt, in another page, to avoid the conclusion,

---

* Pref., p. xxxi.

† Proved to be incredible in "Leslie's Short and Easy Method with the Deist."

‡ Pref., p. xxxv.

that the writer of the Pentateuch *must* have been a bad man if he has indeed recorded ideological falsehoods as historical facts, adding to the record the solemn affirmation—" Thus saith the Lord." Dr. Colenso is quite ready to believe that " in writing the story of the Exodus, the Scripture writer may have had no *consciousness* of doing wrong."* We presume he would persuade us, in the words of one of the Essayists, that " our sense of any difficulty arises only from our modern habits of thought, and from the *modesty of assertion* which the spirit of true science has taught us!"† But in neither case will the bishop's plea avail him anything. Without discussing ancient " habits of thought," we are assured of this, that a narrative, *purporting to be one of positive facts*, which is wholly, or in any essential or considerable portion untrue, can have no connection with the DIVINE REVELATION of a God of Truth. So, whatever may be said of Christ's limited and defective knowledge as man, *His endorsement of a delusion, attributing* DIVINE *authority to a book of historical falsehoods, would utterly preclude our receiving that book as* GOD'S *Book, or recognising Christ Himself as a Teacher sent from God.* We can quite understand, that, as man, Christ's growth in "*ordinary*" knowledge was gradual—that He "increased in wisdom" as well as in " stature :" but we are not now speaking of *ordinary* knowledge. *We are speaking of knowledge which could not be defective without involving the sacrifice of Divine faithfulness and truth.* " Whether the deception be ascribed to ignorance or fraud is quite immaterial, as far as the question of a DIVINE REVELATION is concerned."‡ If the Pentateuch be not historically true, then Christ's teaching, which is constructed on the hypothesis of its truth, can only be placed, as Dr. Colenso seems prepared to place it, on a level with the teaching of Cicero, the Sikh Gooroos, Lycurgus, Numa, Zoroaster, &c.,§—it is entirely bereft of that Divine authority which a written Revelation from God would possess. If the Bishop of Natal has lost faith in Moses, he cannot consistently retain faith in Jesus.

But we may give another, and, if possible, still more decisive answer to this monstrous theory which Dr. Colenso has broached.

* Pref., p. xvii.   † Essays and Reviews.   ‡ *The Record.*   § Pref., p. xviii.

It is true Christ was man, but He was no less truly GOD. Who then shall attempt to separate the action of the human from the Divine mind in our Lord's person? Admitting that, as man, He "grew in wisdom," can we conceive for one moment that, as God, He could possibly fall into error? "*Advancing* knowledge—be it in Paradise, or among the angels who are still but finite, or in that sacred infancy which was passed in Galilee,—does not involve *mistaken* knowledge, much less liability to positive error and deception." But we cannot really separate the human from the Divine. Not to intrude into the mystery of the two Natures in the One Person, we hold, beyond doubt, that throughout the whole of our Lord's earthly ministry there was present in His mind the whole mind of the Father and the whole mind of the Spirit. He knew who wrote the Pentateuch, and whether it were inspired or no. When He declared that He came to "fulfil the Law and the Prophets," He meant by the law what the phrase always meant among the Jews, the writings of Moses. Had the law (which includes the history) been a tissue of mistakes, exaggerations, or interpolations, He, who corrected the misinterpretations of the moral code, would not have left glaring mis-statements of history, prejudicial to the spread of the Gospel in after times, without correction also. Even the Apostles had "the promise of the Spirit" to "guide them into all truth." Had not He who gave that promise the same Spirit? Did He not "know from the beginning who they were that believed not, and who should betray • Him?" (John xi., 65.) Are we not told that He "knew what was in man, and needed not that any should tell Him?" (John ii., 25). And yet, are we to believe that He was ignorant of the character, whether authentic or fictitious, of the Sacred books ascribed to Moses, "the Prophet like unto Himself"—(surely like in *truthfulness*)—who went before Him? (Deut. xviii., 15.)

"If, when Christ began His work, with all the fulness of the Holy Ghost dwelling in the God-man, and with all the Omnipotence of Deity waiting to avouch His doctrine, He who was Himself ',the Truth' as well as 'the Way' and 'the Life,' *could* be in error as to the very foundations of His preaching, and was as liable to mistake the Scriptures of the Old Testament as 'any other devout

Jew of that day'—then, verily, His veracity is a figment, faith in Him is folly, and the God of Truth must be supposed, in the miracles He performed in evidence of His Mission, to have made bare His Holy Arm to set His seal upon error and falsehood!"

This is plain language, but it does no more than state the fearful alternative which Dr. Colenso's present position places before him. Either he must retrace his steps, and acknowledge that the testimony of Christ to the Divine Inspiration and Authority of the Pentateuch as a part of the Old Testament, is decisive and final, or he must impugn the veracity of Christ and reject Christianity as a Message sent from God!

IV.

PRACTICAL BEARINGS OF THE SUBJECT.

It now only remains for me to commend to my readers THE PRACTICAL BEARINGS of the subject of this pamphlet.

The topics which have engaged our attention :—Bible Inspiration—the truthfulness of Old Testament history—the veracity of Him whose Name we bear—have indeed been solemn topics. I trust the discussion of them has been conducted in the spirit of earnest, truth-loving, truth-seeking sincerity. I trust that it has been manifest that my object has not been " controversy for controversy's sake." I trust I have been enabled to rise above the influences of mere controversy, and to realise the momentous importance of the questions at issue.

I am most anxious, in conclusion, to impress, if possible, still more deeply upon the mind of every reader, the consideration of this PERSONAL and PRACTICAL interest, which pertains to each, and is inseparably connected with the enquiry, " Has God spoken? Do we possess a Revelation of His Mind and Will?"

These pages will probably fall into the hands of some, who are verging on the precipice of scepticism and doubt. Let me offer them a friendly word of counsel.

I might say,—Beware of "the evil heart of *unbelief*," excusing sinful habits, and putting away the unwelcome thought of responsibility and a judgment to come. We know there *are* men who fret under the moral restraints of Christianity : who are provoked by its solemn warnings against sin : who are offended by its humbling and self-denying character. But this is not the case with all. There are doubters who are not, in this sense, unbelievers : they do not reject the truth simply because they *wish* it not to be the truth ; but they have allowed themselves to come within the circle of sceptical influences, and they are being *gradually* drawn into the whirlpool of avowed unbelief. It is to these I address myself. I appeal to the honest doubter's better self ; and there are *two thoughts* which I would especially suggest to him.

I ask him, first, to *ponder well the* CONSEQUENCES *of unbelief— to estimate the* LOSS *which he is incurring, by the rejection of the Bible as God's Revelation of His Will to man.*

Let him remember,—" It is the Bible or it is no Bible :" for there is no other book under heaven, claiming Divine Authority, whose pretensions are, for one moment, worthy of examination. He may, with Dr. Colenso, talk of " the Voice of God in the heart,"—of the promptings of the natural conscience within him,—of the sufficiency of reason without Revelation : but, whilst I would not deny that these *may* cast some *faint* rays of light upon the path even of the poor heathen,—whilst I fully recognise the province of reason to weigh the evidences, external and internal, which prove the Bible to *be* a Divine Revelation,—I have the testimony of universal experience, that this light of nature *never* led to the knowledge of the One true God : and I confidently affirm, that the men who, in our own land, exalt reason and conscience as the supreme guides in matters of religion,— ignoring the fact that the one has been darkened and the other blunted and perverted by the Fall,—have really been indebted to the BIBLE they traduce for *every particle* of the religious knowledge which seems to separate and distinguish them from the heathen. They have climbed by means of the ladder of the Bible to the eminence they occupy, and it is vain for them to maintain that they have soared thither on the wings of reason. They *may* imagine that had they been born in the centre of Africa, or on one of the lonely islands of the Southern Sea, they would have been as enlightened as they are now :—but no one, besides themselves, will believe it. We appeal from imagination to fact. Can a single instance be adduced of men arriving at the knowledge of the general truths of religion, apart from Revelation? Can a people be named, unblessed with the light of Bible truth, who have ever grasped, and held fast, the true notion of God? We need not confine ourselves to nations sunk in barbarism and ignorance. We need not point to the New Zealander feasting on the slain dead,—the Indian Suttee,—the murderous Thug. We may go to ancient Greece, the land of art, philosophy, and song : —we may go to Athens itself, the very focus of the wisdom of this world,—and before we reach the Acropolis we are confronted with an altar, bearing this startling inscription, "To the UNKNOWN God." *The fundamental truth* of religion is undiscovered by that very reason which, in other matters, had accomplished marvels which will ever command the admiration of the world !

Dr. Colenso *assumes*, that "his belief in the Living God would remain as sure as ever, though not the Pentateuch only, but the whole Bible were removed"—he *assumes* that "it is written on our hearts by God's own Finger, as surely as by the hand of the Apostle in the Bible, that God is, and is a rewarder of them that diligently seek Him." But this is *only* assumption. Let him study the records of Paganism : let him penetrate the thick darkness of heathenism : let him unravel the subtleties of Atheism, Materialism, Pantheism : and surely he will perceive that his assumption is baseless. Were it not so, we might well ask, Why send a Bishop to the Zulus, to Caffraria, or the Zambezi ? The finger of God has written on all the hearts of those wild African races "That He is God, and that He is a rewarder of them that diligently seek Him ;" and, on Bishop Colenso's showing, that is enough—the Christian system is no longer wanted. But who does not know that this Divine writing on the heart produces no moral fruit till the grace that comes with the Gospel quickens it ? Who does not know that the very necessity of Missionary enterprise is a standing proof of the moral helplessness of the world without the revealed truth ? Dr. Colenso seeks to console himself, in the midst of his doubts and misgivings, by the reflection, painfully significant in its anticipation—"*Should all else give way beneath me,* God's everlasting arms are still under me. I am sure that the solid ground is there, on which my feet can rest in the knowledge of Him." We rejoice in this assurance that he still holds fast the Being of God, and a moral retribution of some kind—for this belief may possibly, through the teaching of the Spirit, lead him back into the clear light—but at the same time, we tell him, that even this limited creed rests on the foundation of the knowledge he has derived from the BIBLE ; and in rejecting the claims of the Bible as God's Revelation to man, he is rejecting that which alone can give authority to *any* creed—that, *without which*, the natural mind would be for ever left to its own vain speculations, "feeling after God" but failing to "find Him."

No! Reason must sit at the feet of the great Teacher : Conscience must be awakened to spiritual sensibility by the Divine Spirit: or man, the heir of immortality, is like a mariner prosecuting a perilous voyage across the pathless ocean, without chart, or compass, or pilot. Take away the Bible, and the world is but one vast quagmire where there is no standing. Break the rock of Scripture, and there are no stepping stones to "the city which hath foundations, whose builder and maker is God."

Let the disciples of modern thought ponder well the CONSEQUENCES which follow the rejection of the Bible, and test the worth of the SUBSTITUTE which is to supply its place.

The second thought which I would urge upon honest doubters, is this : Before you yield to the influence of scepticism, *be sure you have candidly and impartially weighed* ALL THE EVIDENCES *which attest the Divine authority of the Bible.*

These evidences, writers of Dr. Colenso's School, have almost totally disregarded. They have given no answer to Paley, and in leaving him unanswered, they are, in fact, dumb before all those writers whose gold was melted down in Paley's crucible,—Burnet and Leslie, Locke and Lyttleton, Grotius and Le Clerc, Sherlock and Porteus, Newton and Watson : and last, but not least, the

venerated Sumner.* They have not altered the evidence in the
"Trial of the Witnesses." They have found no flaw in Leslie's
infallible test. They have not made Lardner's "Credibility,"
incredible. They have not *touched* Butler's "Analogy." And,
above all, they have not touched a single one of those minute and
long-concealed coincidences with which the Scriptures abound:
coincidences which only a very industrious *mining* brings to light,
which lie too deep for the eye of the ordinary reader, and which
would never have been discovered had not infidelity provoked
Paley and others to excavate the subterranean galleries in which
they are found; coincidences too numerous and striking to be the
effect of accident, and which, if ingenuity had been subtle enough
to fabricate, that same ingenuity would have been too sagacious
to conceal.†

Let then the body of Christian evidences be candidly and
carefully weighed, and there is no fear of the result.

I do not say, indeed, that even *these* evidences will *force* conviction. There may be causes existing in the doubter, which
effectually bar the door of his *heart*: and we know, "a man
convinced against his will is of the same opinion still." The
Bible humbles man and exalts God, and many hate it as they

* As members of the Church of England, humbled by the spectacle of a
bishop assailing the Book of God, we can yet thankfully remember, that he is
a solitary exception on a roll of names, honourable in the judgment of the Church
universal, for the invaluable services they have rendered as the authors of
standard works on the Christian evidences. And whilst we deeply lament the
falling away of one bishop, we are not, as Protestant Churchmen, pledged to the
unscriptural dogmas of Apostolic Succession (in the Romish sense), or Church
Infallibility. "It is not lawful for the Church"—much less for an individual
bishop of the Church—"to ordain anything that is contrary to God's Word
written." (Article xx.) "As the Church of Jerusalem, Alexandria, and Antioch
have erred; so also the Church of Rome hath erred, not only in their living and
manners of Ceremonies, but also in matters of Faith." (Article xix.) However
painful, no strange thing has happened. Bishops are but men, and they have a
special claim upon our prayers, that, in their high and responsible office, they may
be "illuminated with true knowledge and understanding of God's Word" (Litany),
and be "valiant for the Faith." The late beloved Archbishop of Canterbury well
responded, on the day of his consecration, to a faithful layman who uttered as he
passed by, a prayer that God's blessing might rest upon him—"I *need* your
prayers:" and I am sure there is not a bishop on our English bench who
would not from his heart re-echo that response.

† See Blunt's work on " The Coincidences in the Pentateuch."

would hate an honest friend, who tells them salutary but unpalatable truth. Light is painful to the diseased eye: truth is painful to the diseased heart. The eye may close: the heart may resist. Bible evidence, although strong and multiform, is yet only *moral* evidence. It is not like a flash of lightning which will even force its way through the closed eyelids, and make itself visible :—it will not *rend* its way to the soul. There is evidence enough to satisfy the candid and sincere : there is evidence enough to leave a man morally responsible for his faith : but there *is* a veil too thick for evidence to penetrate. The quotation especially applies to our present subject : "If they hear not Moses and the Prophets, neither will they be persuaded, though one rose from the dead" (Luke xvi., 31).

But I do say, that, "if any man will do the will of God,"— if any man desires to know God's will that he may *do* it—then the investigation of the Christian evidences will be demonstrative to him :—"he shall know of the doctrine" of the Bible, "that it is of God" (John vii., 17).

Finally, addressing all who acknowledge the Divine Inspiration and Authority of the Bible, let me say :—

Be not easily shaken in mind, as to the evidences of this Inspiration and Authority : and

Be not satisfied with anything short of an experimental acquaintance with the saving truth revealed in the Bible.

I.—BE NOT EASILY SHAKEN IN MIND, *as to the Evidences of Bible Inspiration and Authority.*

Objectors always make themselves heard. Dr. Colenso's book has gained the world for an audience : but the world will soon forget his book, and the Church will only remember it as one amongst many impotent attempts to destroy what is indestructible. The Bible has been in the furnace of trial times without number, but it has come forth as gold. The waves of controversy have beat against it, but it has dashed them back in glittering and harmless spray. From age to age the Bible keeps its place as the pioneer of progress, frowning on sin, smiling on virtue, withering hypocrisy, and encouraging the broken hearted to trust in a

Saviour whose blood cleanses from sin. We have no fear for the Bible. "Heaven and earth shall pass away, but the Word of God shall not pass away." Infidelity, scepticism, superstition, rationalistic ideology, the criticism of modern thought, are powerless to touch it. In spite of all, and through all, and above all, God's Word lives on, and will live on, fit type of the immutability of Him whose utterance it is.

"Like some tall cliff that lifts its awful form,
  Swells from the vale, and midway leaves the storm,
  Though round its breast the rolling clouds are spread,
  Eternal sunshine settles on its head!"

And then: II.—BE NOT SATISFIED *with anything short of an* EXPERIMENTAL ACQUAINTANCE *with the saving truth revealed in the Bible.*

Rest not in an unrealizing acquiescence in the truth of the Bible. Be not contented with a faith that lacks the witness of the heart. You may not be able to enter fully into the consideration of the Christian evidences, and the proofs of the genuineness of Holy Scripture, but every believer may test Revelation by the touchstone of experience : and, after all, this is the most simple, the most satisfactory, and the most decisive test. The infidel may laugh at this proof : but the believer would die upon the strength of it. And no wonder! You cannot reason a man out of his conviction of the efficacy of his physician's treatment, when he has *recovered* from deadly disease : so *he* is not likely to be persuaded that the Gospel is "a cunningly devised fable," who has proved it to be "the power of God unto his salvation,"—a power that has raised him from "the death of sin" to "the life of righteousness." In vain will the sceptic object, and the infidel cavil, in the presence of the man who has Bible truth engraved on his heart, and witnessed in his conscience, by the experimental teaching of the Holy Spirit.

I cannot refrain from quoting, as illustrative of this experimental acquaintance with the saving truth of God's Word, a remarkable passage from the "History of the Reformation," by Merle D'Aubigné. He is describing the intense interest excited by the distribution of Tyndale's New Testament, in England, in the year 1526 :—

"In the parsonages and in the convent cells, but particularly in shops and cottages, a crowd of persons were studying the New Testament. The clearness of the Holy Scriptures struck each reader. None of the systematic or aphoristic forms of the schools were to be found there : it was the language of human life which they discovered in those Divine writings; here a conversation, there a discourse ; here a narrative, and there a comparison ; here a command, and there an argument; here a parable, and there a prayer. It was not all doctrine, or all history ; but these two elements mingled together made an admirable whole....Academical explanations were not necessary to those noblemen, farmers, and citizens. 'It is *to* me, *for* me, and *of* me that this book speaks,' said each one. 'It is I whom all these promises and teachings concern. This *fall* and this *restoration*...they are mine. That old *death* and this new *life*...I have passed through them. That *flesh* and that *spirit*...I know them. This *law* and this *grace*, this *faith*, these *works*, this *slavery*, this *glory*, this *Christ*, this *Belial*...all are familiar to me. It is my own history that I find in this book.' Thus, by the aid of the Holy Ghost, each one had *in his own experience* a seal to the truth of the Gospel."*

In connection with this eloquent passage from the history of the past, and as showing the inestimable value of an experimental appropriation of Bible truth *as a preservative from the snares of infidelity and the seductions of false philosophy*, I add the following brief account which Dr. D'Aubigné has given of *his own* final establishment in the truth of Revelation.

"After I had begun to preach Christ, I was so assailed and perplexed on coming into Germany by the sophisms of rationalism, that I was plunged into unutterable distress, and passed whole nights without sleeping, crying to God, or endeavouring by arguments and syllogisms without end to repel the attack and the adversary. In my perplexity I visited Kleuker, a venerable divine at Kiel, who for forty years had been defending Christianity against the attacks of infidel theologians and philosophers. Before this admirable man I laid my doubts and difficulties for solution ;

* "History of the Reformation in England." pp. 359-60.

nstead of solving them, Kleuker replied, 'Were I to succeed in ridding you of these, others would soon rise up. There is a shorter, deeper, and more complete way of annihilating them. *Let* CHRIST *be really to you the Son of God—the Saviour—the Author of eternal life.* Only be firmly settled in this grace, and then these difficulties of detail will never stop you ; the light which proceeds from Christ will dispel all darkness.' This advice, followed by a study with a pious fellow-traveller at an inn at Kiel, of the Apostle's expression, 'Now unto Him that is able to do exceeding abundantly above all that we ask or think,' relieved me from all my difficulties. After reading together this passage, we prayed over it. When I arose from my knees in that room at Kiel, I felt as if my wings were renewed as the wings of eagles. From that time forward I comprehended that my own syllogisms and arguments were of no avail ; that Christ was able to do all by His power that worketh in me ; and the habitual attitude of my soul was to be at the foot of the cross, crying to Him, 'Here am I, bound hand and foot, unable to move, unable to do anything to get away from the enemy that oppresses me : do all Thyself : I know that Thou wilt do it ; Thou wilt even do exceeding abundantly above all that I ask.' I was not disappointed. All my doubts were soon dispelled, and not only was I delivered from that inward anguish which, in the end, would have destroyed me had not God been faithful, but the Lord extended unto me peace like a river. If I relate these things, it is not as my own history alone, but that of many pious young men, who, in Germany and elsewhere, have been assailed by the raging waves of rationalism."

A more interesting, instructive, and momentous narrative, I have never perused. Most clearly do we learn from it, that he who is " strengthened with all might by the Spirit in the inner man," and who is " rooted and grounded in love," though less skilful in argument, is in a far better condition to resist the subtleties of infidelity and scepticism, than he who is stronger in his logic but wanting in the grace of experience. Though the strength of the human intellect, the chain of sound reasoning, and the conclusion of a just logic, have fitly and profitably been employed in elaborate defences of the truth ; yet, after all, it is to the blessing of God on the internal vigour of his own piety, that the believer is indebted for his stability, more than to those outworks which are cast up, from time to time by the ablest defenders of Christianity.

Let the Bible, then, be the food of our souls ! The highest kind of certainty belongs exclusively to those truths which have been demonstrated by experience. Let us be satisfied with nothing short of " the witness in ourselves." In the earnest, eloquent, and impressive words of one in whom intellectual power and spirituality of mind are eminently combined :—" It would be a poor comfort to possess a Divine Revelation, if we did not live upon the truths that it reveals. The deepest homage we can render to the authority of the Word consists in the love of the heart, and in the obedience of the life. Then only do we truly honour it, when it becomes our guide in life and our support in death, when it brightens our sorrows and sanctifies our pleasures, and when we follow it as the beacon star whose steady light shall guide our earthly voyage into the heavenly haven, the rest prepared for the people of God. For this, it must become the joy of the heart, as well as the light of the intellect. The lively oracles *may* be amongst us, and yet without a prayerful faith in the worshipper, the Divine voice within them would be dumb—the letter there, but its living spirit absent. We need a larger faith in the promises, and more earnest supplication for the gift of the Spirit. Then would He teach us His marvellous lessons, and step by step, as along the mystic ladder that stretches between earth and heaven, raise us nearer and nearer to God. The first step is on earth, but the highest will be in heaven."*

I have heard of a copy of the Scriptures preserved in one of our old castles, which belonged more than a century since to the noble owner. At the end of many hundred verses through the volume he has carefully signed his name : and at the close of the volume, in a handwriting evidently tremulous from weakness, dated

* "The Bible and its Critics : the Boyle Lectures for 1861." By the Rev. Edward Garbett, M.A. Seeley and Griffiths, London. An *exhaustive* work, worthy of the name of Boyle, with which it stands connected.

a short time before his death, are these words : " I hereby set my seal to the truth of every promise contained in this book, having found them all realised throughout a long life, in my own happy experience."

Happy experience, indeed ! May every possessor of a Bible who may read these pages, be enabled to bear A LIKE TESTIMONY !

NOTE.—On " *The Human Element in Scripture*." To guard against possible misunderstanding, I deem it well, in issuing a Second Edition of this Pamphlet, to add a few remarks on what has been termed, in these pages, "the Human Element in Scripture." I am most anxious it should be understood, that in asserting the presence of this "Human Element" in the *composition* of the Sacred volume, it is by no means to be inferred that human *error* obtained an entrance in the *original autographs*. We admit, although in a very limited degree, the existence of trifling errors made by translators and copyists, in the *transmission* of the Bible from age to age—errors which legitimate criticism, for the most part, easily corrects; but the presence of "the Human Element" in the *composition* of Scripture, is quite consistent with the infallibility of the original autographs : and we distinctly affirm, that every attempt made by sceptical adversaries of the faith to establish *a single contradiction*, clearly inherent in the autographs and their structure, has utterly failed. *Divergencies*—variations— in the accounts given by different writers of the same events, *may* be pointed out. These we trace to "the Human Element in Scripture," and they create no real difficulty: they are the natural and inevitable accompaniment of a Revelation made through a human medium ; and, in point of fact, they frequently afford the confirmation of a double and triple testimony. It is only such divergence as implies direct contradiction, or the partial falsehood of the statement, which can furnish a real argument against plenary and complete inspiration. This divergence does not exist.

Mr. Birks aptly traces an analogy between "the Human Element in Scripture," and "the Human Nature in the Divine Person of Christ." " The lowly birth, the hunger and thirst, the weariness and sorrow, the human words and looks and tears of the Son of Man, are the means by which alone we obtain a true knowledge of the Saviour, and are able to discern, in its fulness, that love of Christ which passeth knowledge. In like manner, we must attend, thought-fully, and with reverence, to the human features of the written word, in order to discern clearly its wisdom and heavenly beauty, as a series of messages, clothed with Divine authority, from the living God to the children of men." This analogy is most suggestive, and defines the true position of "the Human Element in Scripture."

WORCESTER :

PRINTED BY KNIGHT AND CO., BROAD STREET.